PERCUSSION

HOLIDAY FAVORITES

Solos and Band Arrangements
Correlated with Essential Elements® Band Method

Arranged by ROBERT LONGFIELD, JOHNNIE V̶INSON
MICHAEL SWEENEY and PAUL LAVENDE̶R

T0081639

Welcome to Essential Elements Holiday Favorites! There are two versions of each selection in ̶̶. The
SOLO version appears in the beginning of each student book. The FULL BAND arrangement of each song follows. The
ONLINE RECORDINGS or PIANO ACCOMPANIMENT BOOK may be used as an accompaniment for solo performance.
Use these recordings when playing solos for friends and family.

PLAYBACK+
Speed • Pitch • Balance • Loop

To access audio visit:
www.halleonard.com/mylibrary

Enter Code
3374-0641-4181-3916

ISBN 978-1-5400-2801-3

HAL•LEONARD®

Copyright © 2018 by HAL LEONARD LLC
International Copyright Secured All Rights Reserved

Visit Hal Leonard Online at
www.halleonard.com

00870019

Contact Us:
Hal Leonard
7777 West Bluemound Road
Milwaukee, WI 53213
Email: info@halleonard.com

In Europe contact:
Hal Leonard Europe Limited
42 Wigmore Street
Marylebone, London, W1U 2RN
Email: info@halleonardeurope.com

In Australia contact:
Hal Leonard Australia Pty. Ltd.
4 Lentara Court
Cheltenham, Victoria, 3192 Australia
Email: info@halleonard.com.au

AULD LANG SYNE

PERCUSSION 1
Snare Drum, Bass Drum

Words by ROBERT BURNS
Traditional Scottish Melody
Arranged by MICHAEL SWEENEY

AULD LANG SYNE

PERCUSSION 2
Triangle, Sus. Cym.

Words by ROBERT BURNS
Traditional Scottish Melody
Arranged by MICHAEL SWEENEY

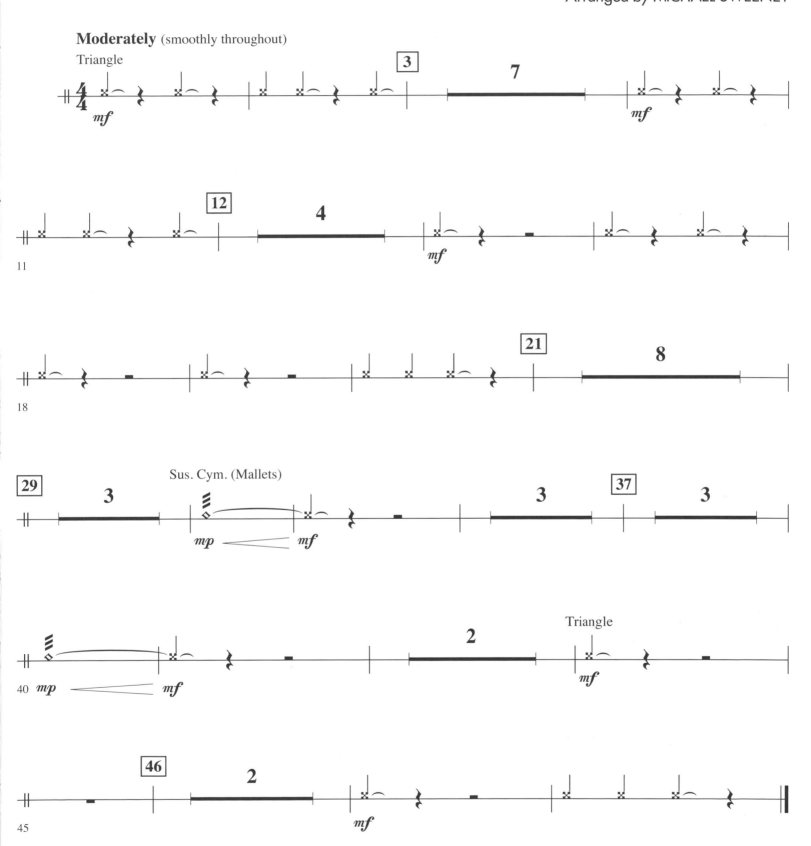

FELIZ NAVIDAD

PERCUSSION 1
Snare Drum, Bass Drum

Music and Lyrics by
JOSÉ FELICIANO
Arranged by PAUL LAVENDER

00870019

FELIZ NAVIDAD

PERCUSSION 2
Guiro or Claves, Sleigh Bells or Shaker

Music and Lyrics by
JOSÉ FELICIANO
Arranged by PAUL LAVENDER

00870019

PARADE OF THE WOODEN SOLDIERS

PERCUSSION 1
Snare Drum, Bass Drum

English Lyrics by BALLARD MacDONALD
Music by LEON JESSEL
Arranged by PAUL LAVENDER

00870019

PARADE OF THE WOODEN SOLDIERS

PERCUSSION 2
Triangle, Sus. Cym., Sleigh Bells

English Lyrics by **BALLARD MacDONALD**
Music by **LEON JESSEL**
Arranged by PAUL LAVENDER

Toy March

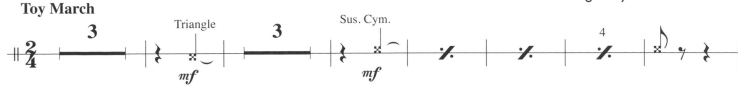

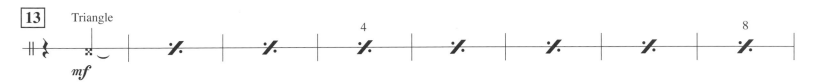

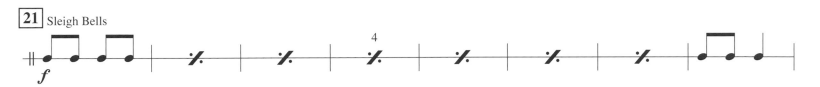

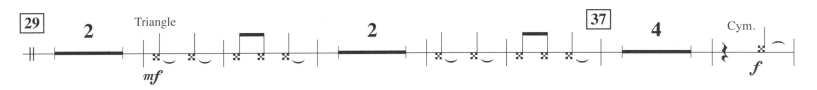

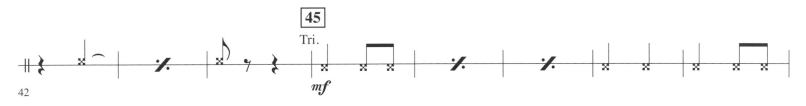

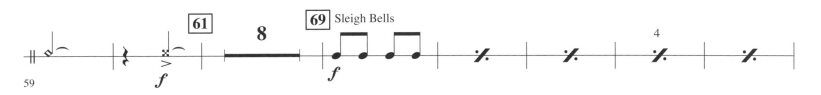

00870019

GOOD KING WENCESLAS

PERCUSSION 1
Snare Drum, Bass Drum

Words by JOHN M. NEALE
Music from PIAE CANTIONES
Arranged by ROBERT LONGFIELD

GOOD KING WENCESLAS

PERCUSSION 2
Tambourine

Words by JOHN M. NEALE
Music from PIAE CANTIONES
Arranged by ROBERT LONGFIELD

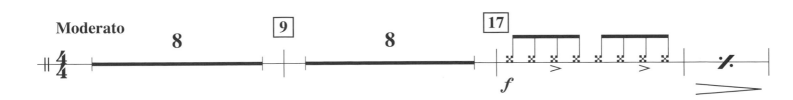

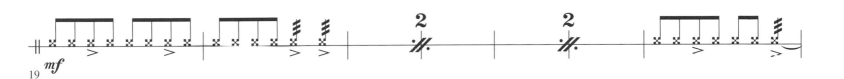

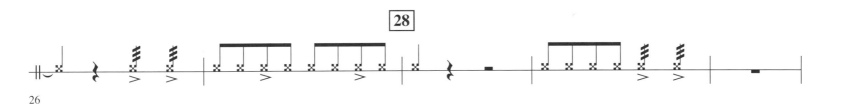

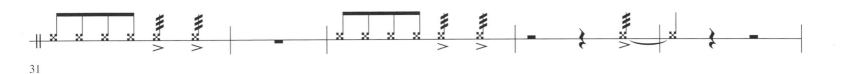

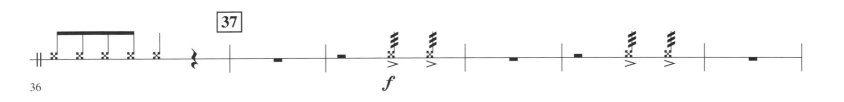

00870019

PAT-A-PAN
(Willie, Take Your Little Drum)

PERCUSSION 1
Snare Drum, Bass Drum

Words and Music by
BERNARD de la MONNOYE
Arranged by ROBERT LONGFIELD

PAT-A-PAN
(Willie, Take Your Little Drum)

PERCUSSION 2
Triangle, Tambourine

Words and Music by
BERNARD de la MONNOYE
Arranged by ROBERT LONGFIELD

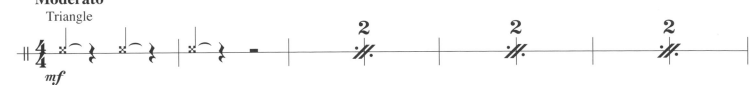

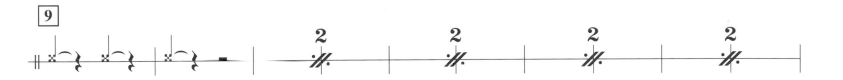

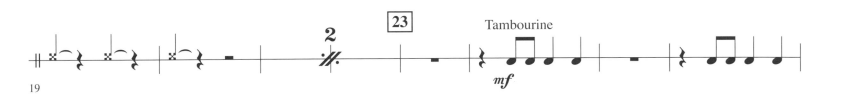

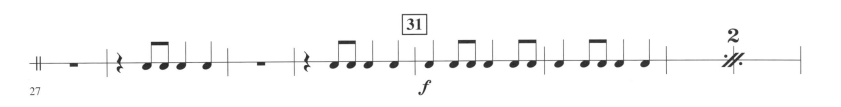

00870019

Silver Bells

PERCUSSION 1
Snare Drum, Bass Drum

Words and Music by
JAY LIVINGSTON and RAY EVANS
Arranged by PAUL LAVENDER

SILVER BELLS

PERCUSSION 2
Triangle, Sleigh Bells

**Words and Music by
JAY LIVINGSTON and RAY EVANS**
Arranged by PAUL LAVENDER

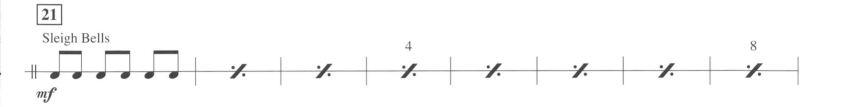

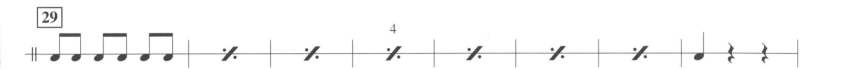

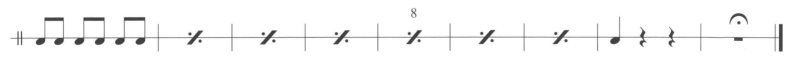

DO YOU HEAR WHAT I HEAR

PERCUSSION 1
Snare Drum, Bass Drum

Words and Music by
NOEL REGNEY and GLORIA SHAYNE
Arranged by MICHAEL SWEENEY

00870019

DO YOU HEAR WHAT I HEAR

PERCUSSION 2

Finger Cym., Sus. Cym., Sleigh Bells,
Triangle, Cr. Cym.

Words and Music by
NOEL REGNEY and GLORIA SHAYNE
Arranged by MICHAEL SWEENEY

00870019

From THE SOUND OF MUSIC

MY FAVORITE THINGS

PERCUSSION 1
Snare Drum, Bass Drum

Lyrics by OSCAR HAMMERSTEIN II
Music by RICHARD RODGERS
Arranged by ROBERT LONGFIELD

MY FAVORITE THINGS

From THE SOUND OF MUSIC

Lyrics by OSCAR HAMMERSTEIN II
Music by RICHARD RODGERS
Arranged by ROBERT LONGFIELD

PERCUSSION 2
Triangle, Sus. Cym.

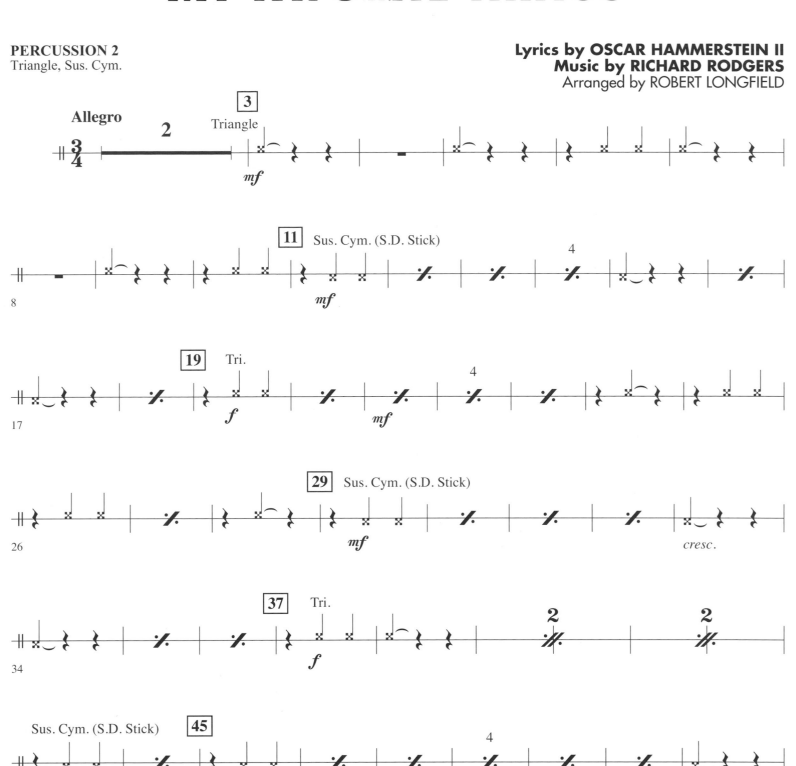

00870019

From the Motion Picture Irving Berlin's HOLIDAY INN

WHITE CHRISTMAS

PERCUSSION 1
Snare Drum, Bass Drum, Ride Cym.

Words and Music by
IRVING BERLIN
Arranged by JOHNNIE VINSON

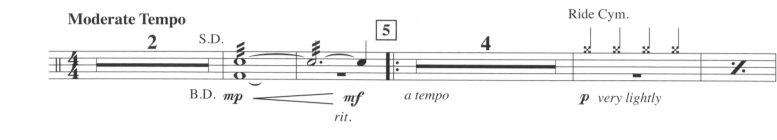

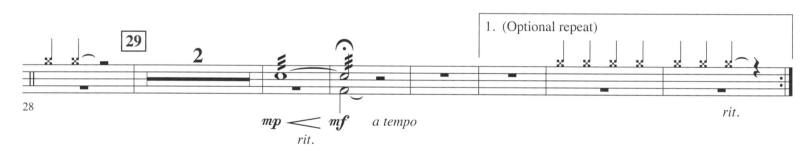

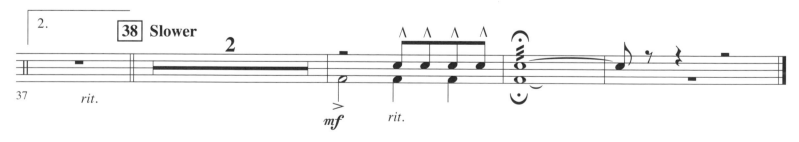

WHITE CHRISTMAS

PERCUSSION 2
Sus. Cym., Mark Tree

Words and Music by
IRVING BERLIN
Arranged by JOHNNIE VINSON

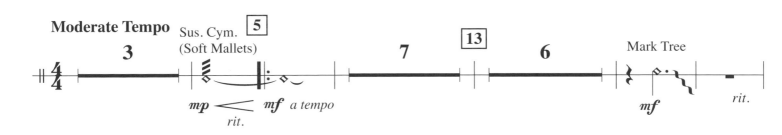

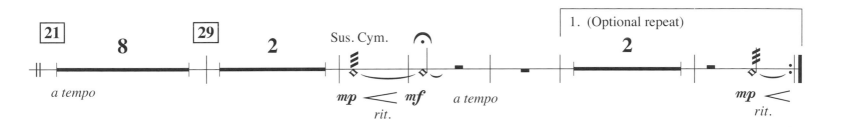

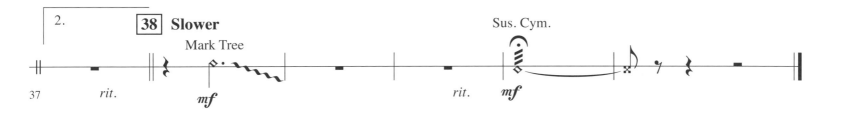

CHRISTMAS TIME IS HERE

PERCUSSION 1
Drum Set

Words by LEE MENDELSON
Music by VINCE GUARALDI
Arranged by JOHNNIE VINSON

Moderately Slow, Smoothly

Christmas Time Is Here

PERCUSSION 2
Triangle, Sus. Cym.

Words by LEE MENDELSON
Music by VINCE GUARALDI
Arranged by JOHNNIE VINSON

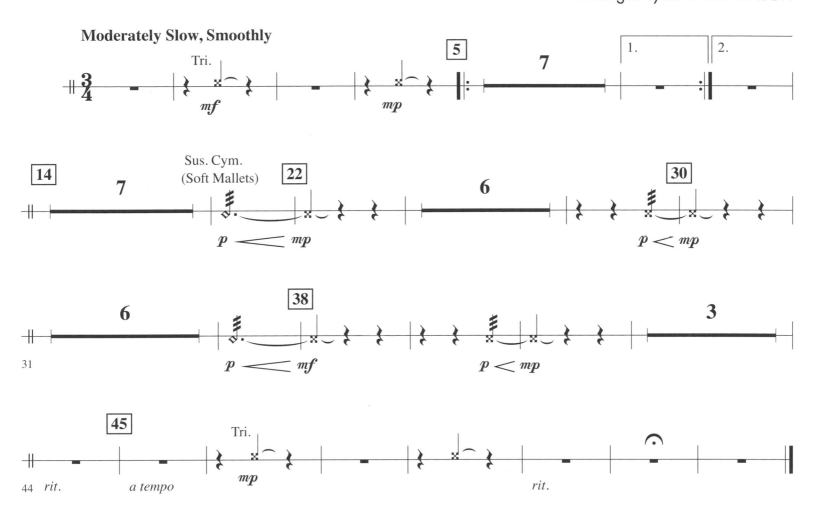

From Warner Bros. Pictures' THE POLAR EXPRESS

THE POLAR EXPRESS

PERCUSSION 1
Snare Drum, Bass Drum

Words and Music by
GLEN BALLARD and ALAN SILVESTRI
Arranged by JOHNNIE VINSON

THE POLAR EXPRESS

Words and Music by
GLEN BALLARD and ALAN SILVESTRI
Arranged by JOHNNIE VINSON

PERCUSSION 2
Hi-Hat, Sleigh Bells

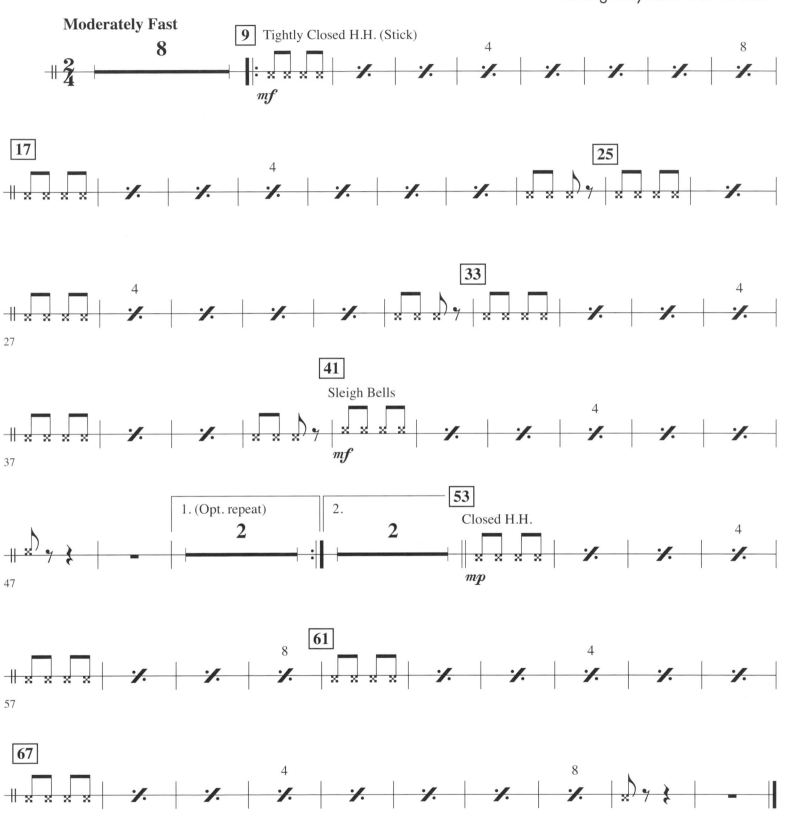

00870019